ANIMALS OF THE AUSTRALIAN OUTBACK

SPEEDY
PUBLISHING

Speedy Publishing LLC
40 E. Main St. #1156
Newark, DE 19711
www.speedypublishing.com

The Outback is the vast, remote, arid interior of Australia. The Outback has no clearly defined boundaries.

The thorny dragon grows up to 20 cm in length and can live for up to 20 years. They're covered from head to tail with spines and thorns. Thorny dragons change color depending on the temperature.

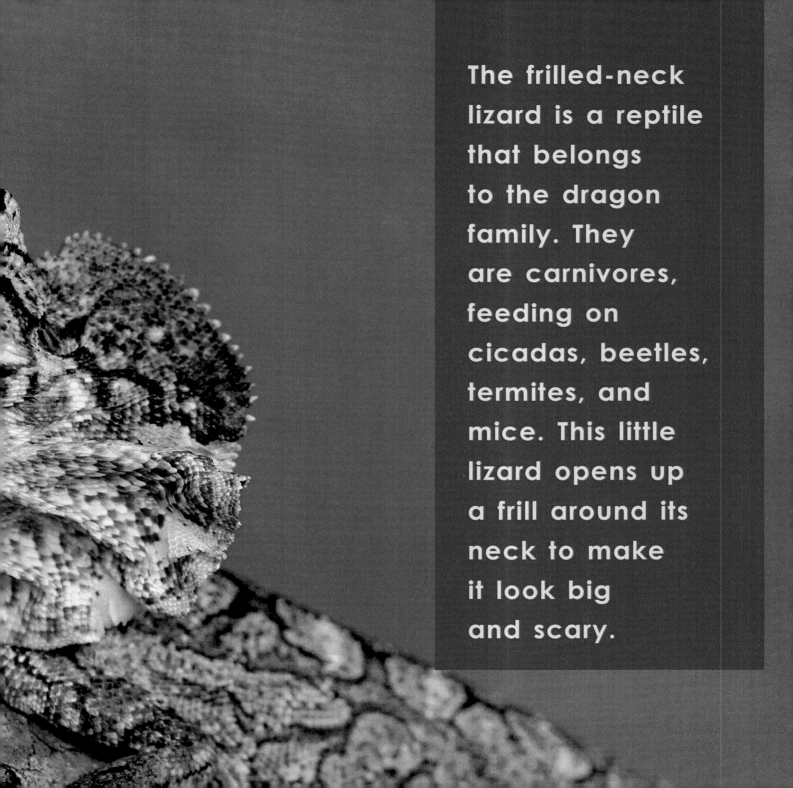

The frilled-neck lizard is a reptile that belongs to the dragon family. They are carnivores, feeding on cicadas, beetles, termites, and mice. This little lizard opens up a frill around its neck to make it look big and scary.

The inland taipan is considered the most venomous snake in the world. It is estimated that one bite possesses enough lethality to kill at least 100 full grown men. Although extremely venomous, this snake is quite a shy and reclusive snake species.

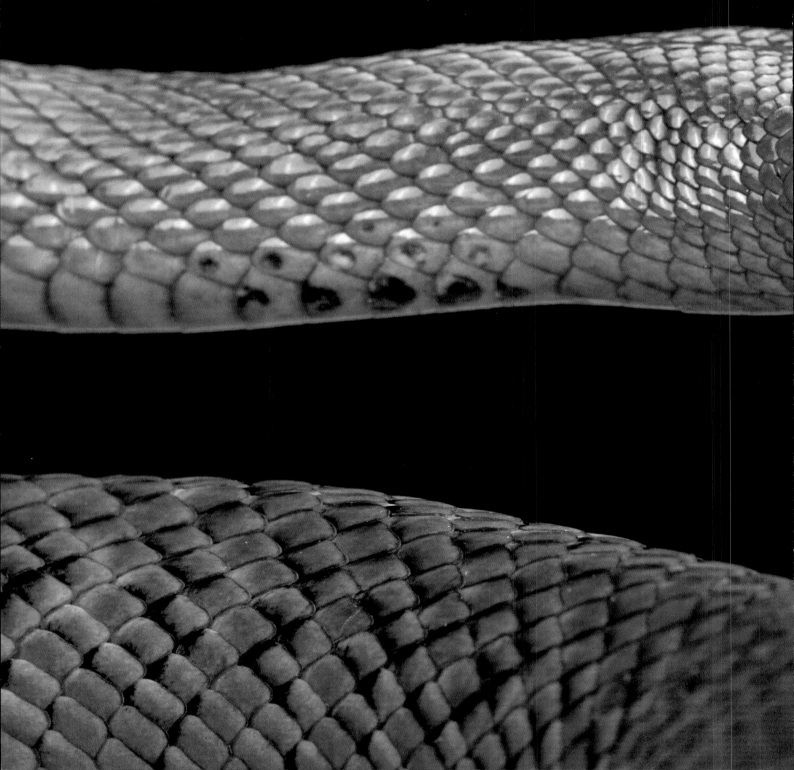

The dingo is a
free-ranging dog
found mainly in
Australia. Dingo
can reach 3.5 to 4
feet in length and
22 to 33 pounds in
weight. Dingoes
hunt mainly at
night. They can
travel 37 miles per
night when they
are searching
for food.

The redback spider is a species of venomous spider indigenous to Australia. Redbacks eat almost any small insects that are caught in their webs. The common name redback is derived from the distinctive red stripe along the dorsal aspect of its abdomen.

Camels were imported to Australia in the 19th century from Arabia, India and Afghanistan for transport and heavy work in the outback. Australia is also home to the world's largest herd of camels. Camels live on average for 40 to 50 years.

The kangaroo is a marsupial with large, powerful hind legs, large feet adapted for leaping, a long muscular tail for balance, and a small head. Kangaroos are endemic to Australia. Kangaroos usually live to around six years old in the wild.

Made in the USA
San Bernardino, CA
03 November 2016